T0146881

NO complaints,
NO outbursts,
POVERTY is not Voluntary.

NO complaints, NO outbursts, POVERTY is not Voluntary.

"An immigrant perspective on
social injustice and social inequality"

MAX CINEUS

Professor of Foreign Languages

No complaints, No outbursts, Poverty is not Voluntary. "An immigrant perspective on social injustice and social inequality"

iUniverse books may be ordered through booksellers or by contacting:

iUniverse
1663 Liberty Drive
Bloomington, IN 47403
www.iuniverse.com
1-800-Authors (1-800-288-4677)

Because of the dynamic nature of the Internet, any web addresses or links contained in this book may have changed since publication and may no longer be valid. The views expressed in this work are solely those of the author and do not necessarily reflect the views of the publisher, and the publisher hereby disclaims any responsibility for them.

Any people depicted in stock imagery provided by Thinkstock are models, and such images are being used for illustrative purposes only. Certain stock imagery © Thinkstock.

ISBN: 978-1-5320-0374-5 (sc)
ISBN: 978-1-5320-0375-2 (e)

Library of Congress Control Number: 2016913598

Print information available on the last page.

iUniverse rev. date: 08/19/2016

If only I could be advocated to express the
viewpoints of the unfavorable classes

ACKNOWLEDGMENTS

THIS BOOK IS MY FIRST INSPIRATION as a writer. I have appreciated the positive and negative criticisms from my readers and especially my students and colleagues who encouraged me to make this dream a reality. I thank iUniverse for their expertise and knowledge in the art of publication.

This book would not have been possible without the support of many people. I wish to express my gratitude to my late mother, Philomene Dorcelon, who passed on July 27, 1997. She was the rainbow of my clouds and the engine of my life. Without her invaluable assistance and care, I would not be in this world, and this book would not have been possible. I love you, Mom, and thanks for bringing me up in this world. *Requiescat in pace.*

I also dedicate this book to my late father, Meres Cineus, whom I never met because I was about four years old when he left this world. May his soul rest peacefully!

My family guided me to light. My wife, Edith Cineus, gave me a life of love and sincere affection. To Kesha and Edwin, our two great kids, are always there to inspire in us joy, happiness, and sincere advice. I want to express my love and gratitude for their understanding and endless love through the completion of this book. I give special kudos to my siblings. I am referring to my dear sisters, Iphigenie and Arlette, whom I love from the bottom of my heart.

Lastly, I offer my regards and blessings to all of those who supported me in any respect during the completion of this book. I wish to give reverence and thanks to all my students and the most caring and outstanding teacher in the profession, Mrs. Linda Westbrook.

This book was designed for use in courses that focus on the economics of development in Africa, Asia, Latin America, Caribbean, and the "transition" countries of East Europe and the former Soviet Union now classified as developing countries. It is structured and written both for students who have had some basic training in economics and those with little or no formal economics background.

INTRODUCTION

THIS BOOK IS THE VIBRANT SOUND bell that starts ringing to alert the poor people that there is hope for them and that their sufferings are not everlasting. A miracle from heaven is still possible to change egoism and hatred in this world.

This book examines how the concept of poverty has developed. What accounts for its persistence, and what measures can be taken to eliminate or reduce it? What is poverty? Poverty is a lack—for example, of food, money, clothing, decent housing, education, material possessions, and even friendship and good relationships with others.

We are living in a perplexing world in which abject poverty afflicts about one-fifth of the world's population. The poor people do not revolt. They have chosen instead some ways to adopt, survive, and cope with their current situations. They are very resilient, and they never raise their voices to question, "Why not a better life?" To fully understand the concept of poverty, it's necessary for one to have experienced it for a long time and to have endured its atrocities.

The United Nations Food and Agriculture Organization estimates that about 795 million people of the 7.3

billion people in the world were suffering from chronic undernourishment in 2014–2016 and that many others had died of chronic illnesses.

In the United States, people can choose from a lot of products when they go to the supermarket. If they have money, they can buy a lot of food, and if they don't have funds, they have vouchers to buy healthy food, including fresh meat, fruits, vegetables, and dairy products. Most Americans do not know the meaning of hunger, because they have more than enough to eat.

We should all agree that hunger is one of the greatest and most important problems in the world. Starvation is a crucial problem that needs to be solved. Otherwise we cannot pretend that our world is fair and provides to all the people the fundamental right to live in pride and dignity. The main reason for hunger is the disproportionate distribution of goods in the world and human egocentrism. To save children from famine, humanity as a whole should stand as one to eradicate poverty.

Haiti is a typical example when referring to the concept of poverty in Third World countries. In 2010, a brutal earthquake that negatively changed the lives of millions of Haitian citizens devastated Haiti. Why does a country in North America have to be on the verge of collapse because of abject poverty? Why do a billion people have to be hungry around the globe?

Wealth is not well distributed in our world. In some countries in our hemisphere, there are plenty of resources to feed humanity as a whole. If sincere charity really prevailed and if the notion of sharing resources with the poor were not a parameter of lies, we would not have seen so much abject poverty, dependency, and deceitful humiliation in the universe, and no nations in the world would have experienced hunger, thirst, and chronic illnesses.

"All for one, and one for all" should be the leitmotif that society should embrace to mollify our attitude toward one another. Ronald Reagan famously said, "We fought a war on poverty, and poverty won." This statement has been socially and historically true.

According to Dwight D. Eisenhower,

> Every gun that is made, every warship launched, every rocket fired signifies in the final sense, a theft from those who hunger and are not fed, those who are cold and are not clothed. This world in arms is not spending money alone. It is spending the sweat of its laborers, the genius of its scientists, and the hopes of its children.

In this millennium, the prime objectives should be to reduce poverty and hunger so people could satisfy their own basic needs, such as nutrition, health, lodging, and education. Are there enough resources on earth for the 7.4 billion people that live on this planet? One could answer with a big yes. Why could this not be a reality? The answer would be "We don't know." Dom Helder Camara wrote in *Essentials Writings*, "When I give food to the poor, they call me a Saint. When I ask why the poor have no food, they call me a communist." On the same lines, Karl Marx argued, "In our society, wealth grows and at the same time poverty grows; the exclusion of lot of people from the existing wealth grows."

India's great moral leader Mohandas Gandhi famously said, "There is enough on Earth for everybody's need, but not enough for everybody's greed." Today, Gandhi's insight is being put to the test as never before.

The United States alone is enough to feed the world three times over. Although there are enough resources in the world for everyone to have a sufficient amount, some people always want to pull the blanket to their side through greed and egocentrism, and they do not share equally their wealth and resources. In this scheme of egocentrism, the poor is getting poorer, and the rich is getting richer. One can assert that hatred from the dominant class has created our world's social unbalance and political instability.

Life is unjust/unfair, although humanity was created just, fair, and honest by the creator of the universe. We the people must be accounted for all of the evils of this world besides Satan, the great corruptor of humankind. More than half of people in the world are starving. Lack of commodity is not solely responsible for this phenomenon; rather it is our greed, selfishness, and self-absorbed ideology to enrich ourselves without any consideration for others.

In an article dated August 30 by David Lazarus of the *Los Angeles Times*, Gina Rinehart, one of the richest cook women in the world, argued, "If you are jealous of those with more money, don't just sit there and complain. Do something to make more money yourself—spend less time drinking and socializing and more time working."

Poor people are not always procrastinating, and they are not jealous of the rich people's privileges. Some people would like to work hard to become successful, but there is no job available to them due to constant recession and crisis in the market. Eli Khamarov wrote, "Poverty is like punishment for a crime you didn't commit."

John Berger said,

> The poverty of our century is unlike that of any other. It is not, as poverty was before, the result of natural scarcity, but of a set of priorities imposed upon the rest of the world by the rich. Consequently, the modern poor are not pitied ... but written off as trash. The twentieth-century consumer economy has produced the first culture for which a beggar is a reminder of nothing.

According to 2011 data released by the U.S. Census Bureau, 15 percent of individuals in the United States live below the poverty line. While down from 15.1 percent last year, it remains statistically unchanged and near a record high. Today, more than forty-six million people live in poverty in America, more than at any point in the country's history.

However, compared to the poorest countries in the world, the poverty rate in the United States is relatively modest. In some countries, the poverty rate is more than five times the current figures in the United States. In Haiti, 77 percent of residents, the highest in the world, live in poverty.

The presence of extreme poverty usually coincides with significant obstacles, including limited resources, disease, famine, and war. *24/7 Wall St.* analyzed how the most impoverished nations ranked in several key areas, ranging from level of peace to economic stability, health, and education. The poorest countries consistently performed poorly in nearly every case.

Educational attainment and literacy rates are particularly low in these countries. While adult literacy figures were unavailable for many of these nations, those that have reported data were among the worst in the world. In several cases, less than half of eligible children were enrolled in primary education, the equivalent of elementary and middle school. In the Democratic Republic of the Congo, listed among the poorest countries, less than a third of the relevant population was enrolled in primary education.

After many years of teaching in various institutions in North America, I acquired many years of experience and many other privileges. In my work environment, some of the staff is very courteous, but some did not even answer to simple greetings such as good morning and displayed a moody face when they have been approached for questions regarding the same work we are all condemned to do. My passion for teaching has helped creating and excellent rapport with all my students.

The American school system is great, but several things need to be changed before reaching perfection. In the Caribbean, an educator is a very revered figure. Students and parents both have cordial respect toward teachers and school personnel as well. Nowadays the concept of respect has gradually disappeared, and some parents seemed resigned from their parental mission, which is assuring a better future for their offspring.

In some Third World countries, children go to school hungry, others go barefoot, and they do not have money to buy basic school materials such as pens, pencils, and notebooks. Teachers also experience similar problems, and they have sometimes worked an entire year without having a salary commensurate with their performance.

Teachers and administrators of the school system are rarely well trained for the job or attend adequate training to raise their educational standards. Poor children are often the brightest ones. They lack so much that some don't even finish elementary school, and they drop out to do dirty work like domesticity and washing cars in the streets.

As an apostolic advocate for the proletarian class, I have always opposed exploitation, injustice, oppression, and political dominances.

I feel that it's downright criminal to suffer and die senselessly and needlessly when others have the resources to do something that can change their fate. Too many kids have died from hunger and starvation in the world, especially in my homeland of Haiti.

In many countries in the Caribbean, children are hungry. They walk nude in the streets not because they are hot but because their parents cannot afford to buy them clothes. Many children stay in the streets every day because they do not have access to proper education. As a result, some of the upper class use them to do domestic work at their residences, which, in my opinion, is a truly vivid example of slavery and human indignity. The Haitian palace looks shiny while the proletarian class reflects an abject dark color of poverty.

Poverty is one of the most urgent issues of our era. I grew up in Haiti, a poor country geographically located in the Caribbean Sea. My observation of misery and abject poverty was alarming, and I felt miserable to visualize a crucial situation without having enough power to help.

By definition, poverty is a state of incapacity of a person to be fully integrated in the normal standard of living of the people in that society because of lack of income, food, and nonfood items for a normal living. In Haiti, this definition of poverty is visible on every corner of the territory, especially after the earthquake that reached 7.0 on the Richter scale struck Haiti on January 12, 2010.

Because of this earthquake, Haiti became more dependent on other nations to reconstruct the country. The Haitian economy is so low that many starving people are rebelling against their government for food and even threatened to destabilize the executive power if their conditions remain stable.

This definition of poverty is visible in the streets of Cuba and many other Caribbean countries. In Cuba, there is an acute housing shortage, crumbling housing, and inadequate supply of water, along with a lack of aspirin, antibiotics, and vitamins, even in the capital, Havana.

I assume that poverty can be caused by lack of capital, food, clothes, and so forth. Also failures in the market system, disappointments from government policies, and discrimination in the markets against the poor can cause poverty. According to Roch Nicholas, there are two groups of people in our society, "Those who have more food than appetite, and those who have more appetite than food." Mahatma Gandhi said, "There are people in the world so hungry, that God cannot appear to them except in the form of bread."

Poverty divides families, communities, and nations. It causes instability and political unrest and fuels conflict. When people are living in poverty, they cannot get the things they need like food, medicine, and clothing. Sometimes they get so desperate they will not hesitate to steal things that do not belong to them.

Why do some children turn to drugs? Sometimes young people growing up in poverty turn to drugs because they feel there is no other way for them to get a better life. Many times they ignore that there are other options out there for them to create a better future. Kids turn to drugs for many reasons, specifically because they want to feel good, there's a lack of fun activities, they want to feel like adults, they desire to get rid of problems, and they experience peer pressure.

Most of the kids in the world grow up without proper guidance, role models, and adequate family supervision. Kids always tend to follow the steps of their parents in the early age, especially during adolescence. The parents' line of conduct often impacts their kid's mind and behavioral patterns. A parenting class should be an integral part of each school curriculum as well as courses related to steps of becoming good citizens and fervent patriots.

Schools in Third World countries have become traumatizing for many poor children and adolescents, along with their parents and teachers. At the same time, school remains a dream that will link them to better life. For instance, many students in Haiti cannot attend because they must help their parents in their garden. Many students cannot go to school because their parents do not have the funds for the obligatory school uniform and books. In the Caribbean, for example, some children need to pay the school fees, and they need money for basic school items. And if they come to school without them, the teacher punishes them.

In contrast to the situation of youth in industrialized countries, here are some of the reasons why many kids in the world, effectively more than one hundred million, do not attend school: poverty, child labor, school tuition, family duties, and lack of schools. Muhammad Yunus, a Bangladesh economist wrote, "If we had believed that poverty is unacceptable to us, and that it should not belong to a civilized society, we would have created appropriate institutions and policies to create a poverty free-world." This statement is not fallacious because our world could be better if earth resources were well distributed and charity could be a prevailing entity of generosity and pity toward one another.

Despite poverty, Haiti is rich in folklore, art, music, and carnivals where people wear a diversity of colors and celebrate in the streets. The Haitians put aside their hunger, and they dance, drink, and enjoy themselves during the three days of carnival in order to forget their frustration.

Dance is an act deeply rooted in the Haitian culture. The music of Haitian culture is varied. The styles of music are Kompa, Twoubadou, Contre-danse, Racine, Cadence rampa, bougi, rara, and voodoo. The following is an example of the cultural events that Haitians call carnivals.

Victor Hugo, a French thinker, wrote, "Music expresses that which cannot be said and on which it is impossible to be silent." Haitian carnival music expresses the joy of the people, their anger against poverty, and their frustration against the government, one that is usually corrupted and did not often care about the welfare of its own citizens who are hungry.

The root of poverty is very clear. If the government is not to blame, it is the people's fault in voting unqualified and corrupted senators and presidents to represent them. Over the years Haiti has become a country that has been suffering under harsh conditions, kidnapping, and lack of organization, and the past dictators have done nothing spectacular to help improve Haiti's horrific status.

Haiti's poverty has pushed its citizens to the extremes because the way of living is inhumane and the level of poverty has gone rampant on a daily basis. When I was a child, I saw many children wandering in the streets starving, and they looked very weak due to malnutrition. Many children in Haiti walk nude in the streets. They walk barefoot and have no one to turn to since the majority of them are orphans or their parents are too poor to come to their rescue.

The poor people in Haiti are so destitute that they always wanted to escape or immigrate to United States, the Bahamas, Dominican Republic, or Cuba. In general, most of the people of the Third World countries continue to suffer poverty as a result of malnutrition, war, AIDS, and lack of jobs for the people to get a salary.

Poverty is a challenge in Haiti and most of the countries in Africa and the Caribbean. The rate of unemployment is high in these places, and their government in most cases is corrupt and weak. I feel that poverty exists because power has been misused by the people in position of power who have refused to provide adequate assistance to the people in need. Many Haitians took to the street last week to strike against their government because they are hungry. Aristotle was right to argue, "The mother of revolution and crime is poverty."

According to statistics, there are 7 billion people in the world. There are about 925 million hungry people in the world, about 13.1 percent of the total. Poor nutrition accounts for 5 million child deaths each year. Geographically, more than 70 percent live in Asia, 26 percent are in Africa, and 4 percent reside in Latin America and the Caribbean. Should people be blamed or be responsible for their own poverty status? According to Andrew Cherchin of Johns Hopkins University, "Americans tend to think of people as being responsible for their own economic woes."

Nobody should be blamed for being poor because they are not always responsible for their own poverty. For instance, for the person who lost his job or was not properly educated, should he or she be responsible for not being able to afford high school tuition to obtain a proper education or lose out on a job?

I assume that the answer is no. When a situation like this occurs, the person has to struggle to find another job, and sometimes the process leads to frustration in which the individual may turn to violence and crime. Most of the poor children who grow up in a poor households have turned to violence and crime just because their basic needs have not fully been satisfied.

In America, most of the voters tend to vote Democrat because they believe the Democrat Party is more lenient toward the poor than the rich. The ten poorest states in the country are mostly Republican with Mississippi as the poorest, followed by Arkansas, Tennessee, West Virginia, Louisiana, Montana, South Carolina, Kentucky, Alabama, and North Carolina. The ethnic group in these states are mostly white. Why do these poor people always tend to vote Republican? This question remains to have an answer.

Karl Marx defines social class as a large group of people who rank close to one another in terms of wealth, power, and prestige. Also according to Marx, there are two groups in social class: capitalists who own means of production and workers who sell their labor.

The pyramid above depicts the flagrant inequality among ethnic groups and social classes. As one may look at it, the masses lie down way below this pyramid due to economic deprivation and low social classes. Inequality sometimes can be a factor of social conflict and violence. In Haiti, there is a constant and continual conflict among social classes because the riches hold the means of production, and they use their economic power to crush the masses. Some sociologists argue that social inequality is good because, without social inequality, it would be difficult to divide labor among the social groups.

Poverty and Violence

Mary McCarthy said, "In violence we forget who we are." Any person who is hungry often has some difficulties in controlling his or her temperament and maintaining a constant normal behavior pattern. We are often a different person when we are hungry. Hunger can push someone to steal and be belligerent, especially against those who control the means of production. Bill Cosby once wrote, "The main goal of the future is to stop violence. The world is addicted to it."

In order for violence to be decreased, people should have all their basic needs satisfied, and the attitudes of all the people in our universe must be improved in terms of relationships toward one another. Violence has many causes. It can be manifested by frustration, anger, exposure to violent television shows, violence in the home or neighborhood, and some other hostile behaviors. Certain factors also increase the risk of aggression, such as drinking, arguing, provocations, as well as some environmental factors like heat and so forth.

Everywhere in the world, violence goes rampant, and almost every day, some bad news about death is unfortunately the title in magazines and daily news. Jean Jacques Rousseau once said, "Men were born just, but were corrupted by society." A hatred act is easier to do than the good. Murders, police brutality, unnecessary war, and use of atomic bombs are vivid signs of a generation that is being collapsed. Is this why Mother Nature is in revolt? It is pathetic to see how global warming is affecting our world. We must prepare ourselves for the return of Jesus in order to liberate this world from all the evil and hatred feelings.

Climate and Global Damage

From Alaska to Peru, indigenous people across the world already have to face up to the damage that climate change is imposing on their lands. Due to their reliance on the land—culturally, spiritually, and physically—indigenous people are one of the most vulnerable to climate risks. But campaigners warn against seeing them as one heterogeneous group. From region to region, the difficulties and opportunities posed by climate change differ wildly. While in the Arctic Circle, communities worry over thinning ice. In Peru, communities have to deal with the loss of their rain forests.

World Crucial Problems

According to Glenda Haughian, the most crucial and urgent problems that humanity is facing today are food, education, insecurity, wealth distribution, housing, homelessness, overpopulation, war, health, multiculturalism, racial relationships, sex equality, and the environment. All these problems can be eradicated if the world were united as one and if the spirit of sharing surpassed the one of hatred, selfishness, and money-grubbing.

Haiti used to be one of the best places on earth to live. Although the country is labeled as one of the poorest countries worldwide, many Haitians abroad have felt homesick when living outside the country for a long time. The city was absolutely safe. One could wander anyplace at midnight, looking like a tourist, and not have a thing to worry about. Haiti was clean and once called *La Perle des Antilles* (The Pearl of the Antilles).

Haiti nowadays is the poorest country in the Western Hemisphere and has suffered decades of environmental disasters, political instability, and poverty. Haiti is no longer a tourist destination, and following the 7.0 magnitude earthquake in 2010, which tragically killed over three hundred thousand people, the country cannot now sustain on its own without the help of the international community and Haitian diaspora.

Our world is plunging to its lowest level of decline during the last decade. Nature is maddeningly in revolt because God has been too angry against human senselessness and immaturity. Global warming is a significant sign that our planet is gradually dying, and carbon dioxide, methane, and nitrous oxide have been the causes that would account for its death. Methane is a greenhouse gas that traps heat in the earth's atmosphere.

The demographic explosion also causes global warming on our planet. More people mean more food and more methods of transportation. More people also means more cars, and more cars means more pollution. Also many people have more than one car.

Carbon dioxide is a major contributor to global warming. We breathe out carbon dioxide, and the trees convert our carbon dioxide to oxygen. Many nations cut trees for their homes and buildings, and they are not replacing them. Not only are they killing themselves, but they are also constantly taking advantage of earth's natural resources and giving nothing back in return.

There is a major difference between rich and poor as well as capitalism and socialism. In a socialist system, the state has control of some or all means of production. Capitalism, on the other hand, means an economic system in which all or most of the means of production are privately owned, and the goods and services are sold mainly in a free market rather than by the state. However, almost all modern capitalist countries combine socialism and capitalism.

Socialists believe economic inequality is bad for society and the government is responsible for reducing it via social programs that benefit the poor. Examples include free public education and health care, Social Security for the elderly, and higher taxes on the rich. Some socialist countries around the world are Cuba, Venezuela, North Korea, Vietnam, Syria, Belarus, Sweden, and China.

Capitalism is the system of laissez-faire that is characterized by private ownership of capital goods. This social system now exists in all countries of the world. In a purely capitalist economy, there would be no public schools, state-owned or maintained roads and highways, public works, welfare, unemployment insurance, worker's compensation, and Social Security benefits. Under the capitalist system, a small minority of people own the means of production and distribution, such as goods, factories, technology, and transport. Malcom X said, "You can't have capitalism without racism."

Is Jesus socialist or capitalist? This is a very paradoxical question for philosophers who are interested in the study of existentialism. In Matthews 19:21, Jesus said to the apostle, "If you would be perfect go, sell what you possess and give to the poor and you will have treasure in heaven, and come, follow me." Is this act socialist, capitalist, or both? May God enlighten us to answer this pertinent question.

The true capitalist or socialist system does not exist. We live in a world in which the true system is based on exploitation and personal interest. The concept of equal pay for equal work is a paradigm in almost every country in the world, especially those classified as democratic societies.

No justice can surpass injustice in this world. Life is a fight, but the battle is not against hunger, injustice, poverty, immorality, promiscuity, addiction, natural disasters, discrimination, and racism. It is rather the fight to extend the degree of pauperism to perpetuate slavery and to raise the standard of poverty up to the highest culmination point. A person who works forty hours a week should not be below the poverty line in a country in which the rules of law prevail and human rights are respected. The people living below the poverty line are in fact the ones who work harder but unfortunately bring less money at home to help their family. When a family is being abused in their job, there is mostly lack of food, hygiene, entertainment, happiness, intellectual information, and technology devices, but there is constant fighting among siblings and abject poverty in the household.

Poverty is a very controversial issue. According to the World Bank, approximately 2.6 billion people—or 42 percent of the world population—lived in poverty in 2006. In the United States, the richest nation on earth, more than 14 percent of households were below the poverty line.

Extreme poverty is linked with fewer opportunities for education and quality medical care, higher infant death rates, and rampant crime rates. A meaningful path out of poverty requires a strong economy that produces jobs and good wages; a government that can provide schools, hospitals, roads, and energy; and healthy, well-nourished children who are the future human capital that will fuel economic growth.

Is the end of humanity near? Is the extinction era getting closer? Many people are asking these two questions every day, and apparently their questions are still unanswered. There were six major earthquakes in the last seven years, several tropical storms, weird stories of objects falling from the sky, fire devastation, and many torrential downpours causing severe destructions in many countries in the world. Are all these signs to alert the world to be prepared for an imminent cosmic cataclysm in which God will destroy the ruling powers of evil?

God is the Supreme Being, and he is the only one that knows the answer to this question because he has been recognized as the alpha and omega of humankind, the one that governs the world and remains the sublime protector of humanity.

America is in a recession. The world is in crisis. On October 29, 1929, or Black Tuesday, the stock market crashed. Afterward, the US economy was getting worse and worse. People did not have money to pay their loans. They were losing their jobs and homes, and many people could not provide for their families due to lack of food, money, and commodities.

During the Great Depression, President Herbert Hoover tried to convince Americans that the economy was stable, but the American people did not believe in his words. In the 1932 presidential election, Herbert Hoover was not reelected. Franklin D. Roosevelt (FDR) was elected in a landslide. With FDR, people nourished a new feeling of hope and confidence in the economy.

On March 1933, thousands of people traveled to Washington to watch their new president's inauguration. After his inauguration speech, people became certain that things were going to get better. And after taking office, FDR developed a new economic plan to eradicate the Great Depression. It was called the New Deal, a set of actions that was intended to help the economy when it was in great difficulty. The FDR recession dated from mid-1937 to 1938 when the economy recovery was nearly impossible and the unemployment rate jumped from 14.3 percent to 19 percent. In April 1938, President Roosevelt got $3.75 billion from Congress, which was split among many recovery agencies, and the economy once began to recover. By the end of the 1930s, the United States was out of the Great Depression.

There are many similarities between the Great Depression and the recession we are in now. At the beginning of this recession, our stock market began having out-of-control days. One day it even fell six hundred points. It was northing like Black Tuesday, but it made Americans become very worried. After that, more Americans began losing their jobs, houses were getting foreclosed, and several Americans began to worry about how to provide for their families. Throughout this, President George W. Bush tried to reassure Americans that the economy was stable, but many did not agree.

On January 20, 2009, the day when President Barack Obama was inaugurated, Americans once again felt that same hope and optimism. Shortly after taking office, on February 17, 2009, President Obama signed his Economic Stimulus Package into law.

Many of the things that happened during the Great Depression occurred during this recession, but during the Great Depression, things were a lot worse. The New Deal worked for America back then, and hopefully the stimulus package will work now. We are not out of the recession yet, but many polls are starting to show that many Americans believe we are beginning to improve.

The concept of recession is not a new phenomenon. I have been witnessing recession since I was a child. If the world leaders were really determined to do their jobs, the concept of recession would have been eradicated in this world. A lack of coordinated progress keeps the world's momentum to accelerate toward the right direction.

We are living in a world of promise, and none of our world leaders is really working consciously to set forth liberty, equality, and brotherhood on this planet. Corrupted politicians got to power through lies, promises, and sometimes fraud, and once they had satisfied their greed and ambitions, they forgot their promise.

It's a disgrace, a shame, a betrayal, and an abuse of authority. The perfect world built by God has become a stupid jungle in which all the animals are fighting for their own survival. The world could have been a better place if egotism, hatred, and selfishness were not a passport to destroy humanity and the geophysical sphere that we are all condemned to share or live on.

Elevation of crime rate and severe decline in human morality on our world, income, and wealth are very unevenly distributed, and this leads to the widespread persistence of poverty. Half of humanity is living in abject poverty, shame, and inhumane living conditions. Do we have enough resources here below that could eradicate hunger and deprivation once and for all?

The morality of humanity is at its lowest point, and many of us had forgotten the notion of fraternity and togetherness toward one another. The giant boat that all of us have been sharing is on the verge of sinking, causing the death of all of us. All this will be occurring because of our own selfishness and egocentrism.

Our world is in disarray, and the inhabitants of this planet are very reluctant to change their harmful attitudes and manners that are crushing this society. Everywhere on the planetary system, it's quite impossible to encounter a good Samaritan that is really working to humanize the world and save it from the perilous plunge into the darkness. Nanana Mouskouri, a French diva, wrote, "Wherever you turn, there is always something wrong with the politicians. They have everything they need to save the world, and they don't save it."

Is poverty dishonest? Many people have concerns about their socioeconomic status, and some have considered poverty as a dishonest act. Henry Ward Beecher quotes, "No man can tell whether he is rich or poor by turning to his ledger. It is the heart that makes a man rich. He is rich or poor according to what he is, not according to what he has."

Our efforts to intellectually cultivate ourselves could lead us to a better destiny if the means of production were equally distributed and if there were not too much competition in the job market. A man once asked Diogenes what the proper time for supper was, and he answered, "If you are a rich man, whenever you please; and if you are a poor man, whenever you can."

Poverty is not a dishonest act because no one in life can force himself or herself into poverty. Poor people, however, have rarely shown some smile on their faces. Virginia Woolf argued, "To be caught happy in a world of misery was for an honest man the most despicable of crimes."

In the United States, there should be a set of policy recommendations for increasing access to affordable housing and addressing income equality. Many people are working in the United States, but they cannot afford to pay their rent because their wages are far insufficient to cover all their expenses. It's about time for the system of "equal work for equal pay" stop being a slogan and rather become a fact. Individuals doing the same work should receive the same remuneration, and substantially their jobs should be also equal. People working hard are often the ones who have been less remunerated and exploited. It's quite true to understand that social inequality could account for the existence of what many researchers sometimes refer to as poverty and homelessness. Roman Catholic priests believe that human life is sacred, and they advocate for the dignity of the poor to be respected. If people are more important than things, why do they accord more importance to material things than men?

The U.S. Census Bureau announced that about one in every six children in the United States live in abject poverty. Could we imagine how poverty is in Third World countries and the number of children who are dying hungry on a daily basis? The United Nations should integrate in its mission a policy to reduce spending in nuclear ammunitions and direct the allocation of money to feed the poor around the hemisphere. We all should agree that, in a society marred by deepening divisions between rich and poor, our main priority should be to put the needs of the poor and vulnerable first. The economy of the world must serve all the people around the world because the resources of earth are for all of us, especially those who have nothing. Everyone in life has basic rights that must be respected: the right to get a job, the right to decent and fair wages, the right to proper education, the right to free expression, and the right for fair justice.

The late Pope Paul VI once said, "If you want peace, work for justice." The cause of calamity in the entire world is the fact that men are unjust and fair social justice has been always a myth. We have injustice at home, work, our court system, church, and even our grave. We are one human family, no matter what racial, ethnic, and economic background we come from. The time comes, and the clock is ticking to start protecting people and the planet.

Our social welfare has failed. Our social justice has failed not only across the political spectrum but also the ideological spectrum as well. All Americans should recognize or acknowledge that the American social welfare has been a failure. The government did not do enough to ease the plight of the poor. In my encounter with different students who are unemployed or on welfare, they told me that they were trapped in a system that destroys opportunity for themselves and hope for their children. They all want a new approach to fight poverty because none of the proposals being presented by either conservatives or liberals is likely unable to bring a solution or fix the welfare system.

The system of charity around the world, especially in Haiti, has been a dismal failure because the charity has stayed on top and never gone down where the poor people really needed it. Many people feel that private charity should be stepped up to fill the void. We all agree that a job is better than any welfare program. However, where are the jobs? Many companies have moved to China or Japan to escape high taxes and decrease the rate of labor.

We cannot pretend to solve poverty in the world without bringing forth the failed government-run school system. Most of the world leaders invest more money in buying arms rather than building schools to educate children. American schools are very segregated on the basis of race as well as income. Many middle-class parents prefer to send their children to private schools because of lack of discipline and lack of budget for providing adequate learning materials. Poor people are trapped and forced to send their children to a public school that fails to provide quality education.

Prejudice is a factor that has been influencing false misconceptions about people. In our generation, prejudices against poor people, immigrants, and blacks are obvious. There are other different types of prejudices as well, such as those surrounding sexual orientation, stereotyping, anti-Semitism, racism, and pervasive xenophobia. The immigrants are the engines that boost the economy, but some people are very allergic to immigrants. They even reproach them for somehow creating unemployment—by taking cheap remuneration for a job that should pay more from a certified entrepreneur. In a grim report by Katie McHugh detailing America's severe economic decline, the Associated Press brushes off two crucial factors: mass immigration and Obamacare's grip on employers.

A record 93,626,000 Americans have stopped looking for work in an economy that managed to create only one job for every two immigrants the government let in from 2000 to 2014. When all US job growth goes to foreigners at the expense of Americans, while everyone in the labor force sees his or her wages suppressed year after year, it makes sense that some would throw in the towel and others would tolerate less-than-ideal jobs to make ends meet. American workers used to be about to push for greater economic freedom and better working conditions, as the labor community might remember.

The world economy is taking a downturn, especially in Third World countries such as the Caribbean nations. Let's take Haiti, for example, since it has been the place where I grew up and achieved part of my education. Haiti is geographically located in the Caribbean. Haiti, once known as Hispaniola, used to be a nice and prosperous island. It is the poorest country in the Western Hemisphere but the greatest one considering the poor country's past history.

In Haiti, about 80 percent of the population lives in abject poverty. Half of its population lives in extreme poverty and lives on less than one US dollar per day. About 1.5 million people earn more than two dollars per day. Haiti has been very financially unstable because its currency is gradually decreasing in values corresponding to the US dollar.

The per capita income in Haiti is $500. It's obvious that a country with so many problems would never attend a level of stability, either politically or economically. This economic fragility can be traced to the country's bad governance, laissez-faire, and perpetual corruption. Haitian leaders are all corrupt, and they are so egocentric that they would not hesitate to destroy the entire country to win an election for higher offices.

Haiti's illiteracy rate is about 90 percent, and those who are literate use their knowledge to exploit the proletarian classes for whom they pretend to be working in their rhetoric. About 40 percent of children are begging in the streets. They fail to attend school because their parents are either dead or do not have money to pay for their education. School is a place where a child goes in order to become more mature and productive in life. Because of financial hardships, many young children are forced to become adults and perform the tasks that adults should perform.

Haiti experienced many political crises, especially in the 1990s. All those events contributed to the country's underdevelopment. Haiti is one of the most corrupt countries in the world. Everyone's desire is to enter politics to become a millionaire. Haitian leaders or thugs gain unjustly wealth and leave the masses squelching in the mud. As a result, the innocent poor people cannot even cover their own dietary needs.

The good foundation to a strong society is education, a key that can open any doors and break social barriers. In my dear country, many schools were the targets of violence. Looting and crime forced schools to close for several months. The Haitian government did not create an aid program to help the poor parents educating their children. A good education system must create schools that are more accessible to children. A responsible leader must provide school supplies, uniforms, and food to help the children stay healthy in order to be in good shape to attend classes.

In Haiti, any little thing that is a minimum in other regions of the world is a luxury for some Haitians. The needle of the Haitian government watch is going in reverse, and they are totally blindfolded to the crucial problems that the country is facing. In the last fifty years, due to dictatorship, Haiti ended up with a lot of provisional governments, fraudulent elections, military interventions from the United States, and some severe economic sanctions that devastated Haiti's economic development. No one can forget the dictatorial era of "Baby Doc" as well as the notorious brutal dictatorship of François "Papa Doc" Duvalier.

After lack of money management, brutality, economic oppression and depression, inflation, and political conflicts, many investors stopped visiting Haiti because the country was too unstable politically. Haiti should work side by side with the international community to form a plan for the development of a good educational system.

One of the crucial problems in Haiti is also the environment. The environmental factors engender poverty. In Haiti, the process of deforestation is moving from the suburbs to the capital with an accelerated rhythm. The peasants in the countryside cut trees to make charcoal and build houses. This kind of deforestation has a tremendous impact on the economy. Haiti is a country full of debts. The country borrowed money to import mineral products and buy oil from Venezuela. Haiti depends on international donation and foreign assistance.

Since the poverty level is so high, the hunger level is also the same. As a result, many children died of malnutrition, diseases, and chronic starvation. Haiti, Afghanistan, and Somalia are experiencing the same worst form of poverty, and their situation tends to deteriorate instead of improve. According to many researchers, the causes of poverty in the world are often the long history of political oppression, corrupt leadership, soil erosion, and lack of knowledge and literacy.

Economists reported that Haiti was a prosperous country in the 1750s. It used to import sugar, coffee, cocoa, tobacco, cotton, and indigo to France as well as half of the gross national product (GNP). France has made incredible profits from the island of Hispaniola. Other greedy nations, neocolonialist power, and conservative tendency also perpetrate Haiti's poverty. A country on the verge of progress needs a system of good leadership.

Haiti's people are the nicest ones on the planet. It is a generous country and one that opens the door to whoever has wanted to immigrate. But many countries have returned Haitians back home when misery and financial hardships had forced them to emigrate. Haitians are the best examples of workers in the world, and their love for their country is exemplary. All the Haitians would stay home if their country offered the possibility to do so.

Poverty in Haiti has even an impact on the Dominican Republic. Many Haitians immigrated illegally to take refuge in the neighboring country to escape poverty. The Dominican government has tightened security in order to stop the ongoing influx of Haitian immigrants. The Dominican government is very dependent on Haitian workers because of cheap labor. Many people feel that is a modern-day slavery when they are referring to how they treat their Haitian counterparts.

Haiti is a failed state where only foreign investments could improve the economy. The Haitian sanitation department is nonexistent despite the employers and employees receiving their monthly wages to perform the job of cleaning the streets. People who visited Haiti described it as a dirty place with piles of garbage in the streets and sewage flowing in open canals. Haiti reflects a scene of misery in which people walk barefoot. Political propaganda is spray-painted on the walls. Also many merchants are selling various things such as soap, water, and fried plantains, and they walk around carrying a bucket of water on top of their head.

Many writers would like to say more positive things about Haiti, as they always did in the past, but the truth cannot be hidden. The polluted Haitian water caused deaths, especially in the rural sections of Haiti.

Haiti has many wealthy people and millionaires, but while they are living a conservative life, 80 percent of the population is living in abject poverty. The United Nations estimates that 610,000 Haitian children are orphans. Many writers feel that political instability, poor governance, misuse of public funds, and corruption account for the extent of poverty in Haiti.

As a child who grew up in Haiti, I endured and experienced some good moments of happiness and other atrocious moments of pain and despair. My mother was illiterate, but she was a rock. She had a solid brain that some of the educated parents did not have. My dad died, and I do not remember anything about him. When the funeral was passing, I was crying not for his death, but because my mom got dressed and left me to attend Dad's funeral. I was about the age of four. I did not accompany her when she went to bury my dad.

During my adolescence, I saw many abnormal forms of poverty, abject misery not only in my surroundings but also along the neighborhoods not too far from my home. My mom was a merchant of rice. She was lucky enough to become so prosperous with this kind of commercial activities. Her trade was profitable, and we had to thank God that we never experienced hunger and starvation. Many children, however, did not have such a privilege that I had. I saw children who really live in grinding poverty and starvation.

The roads ahead for these youngsters are paved with pitfalls, especially in rural areas. These children are walking nude and barefoot because their parents cannot afford buying things that they need. Many are orphans, and they use them in domestic capacity without attending elementary school. Many of these children died from chronic illnesses such as HIV, malaria, cholera, and chikungunya due to the lack of safe water. Gandhi wrote, "Poverty is the worst form of violence." This statement is true because those who are hungry can become violent as a response to their hunger.

Haiti is a country in which people live for living with no hope for a better future. People are sick and cannot find medication for their disease. There a few pharmacies, but they likely have enough medication to serve people's needs. Many merchants are selling expired medications in the streets without the local authorities sanctioning them. In the hospitals, I witnessed a lack of medical equipment, doctors, and nurses to take care of the sick people.

There is a high rate of criminality in the country. Almost every hour, a crime is perpetrated on innocent people. One of my cousins has just been the victim of a horrible crime that cost him his life. He was cut all over with machetes, and the murderer has never been found to be brought to justice. There are many cases similar to these ones that have never been reported.

In Haiti, the rate of unemployment is skyrocketing, and it is nearly reaching 50 percent. Many young boys and girls who have graduated from universities are still depending financially on their parents because they have no jobs for them to do. They either got a visa to escape poverty or enter politics to become millionaires through blandishment and misuse of public funds.

The Haitian environment has reached a level of substantial degradation. The country is no longer *La Perle des Antilles*, as it was once called in past years. All of its resources are gone, and the cost of life is going rampant as never before.

The world in general is at a level of declination, and all of the good things on earth are on the verge of vanishing. The birds, the beautiful butterflies, the good shade, the dark blue of the ocean, and the concept of mutual respect from children toward adults are declining, and the ethical values have become inexistent. No one seems to have empathy for others anymore, and one prefers to see another falling instead of rising. Egocentrism leads our humanity toward perversion and lack of dignity to a point that killing each other surpasses the concept of caring for one another, as it was to be back to twenty years ago.

The world is approaching an end because the biblical prophecy has begun to be accomplished. Even Mother Nature seems to be in chronic rebellion against our misdeeds in this world. Children became violent toward parents. The parents themselves failed on their mission to breed their children and assure they became responsible citizens.

If there were cofraternity in this world, starvation would not exist, and there would not be poverty as well. The earth has enough resources for everyone to lead a decent life without frustration and anger. There would be a lot of millionaires than poor in this world. If there were solidarity and generosity, there would be no beggars, sufferings, and distress in the world.

There will be a time in which everything and everyone will collapse into chaos and death. On this day, the power of man will end, and people will surely give more consideration to the glory of God rather than material things they are attached to. The doomsday seems to be imminent, considering how everything is dissolving into chaos and destruction. Many people are unprepared spiritually for the doomsday, and no extension will be granted for sinners who hope they would have time to repent for their sins.

People nowadays care about their own individuality without any consideration of their surroundings. The poor is different in everything from the rich. The poor has nothing in their pockets, but they surely have bigger hearts than the rich do. The rich people do not care about anyone below the economic ladder, except for their wealth, money, and reputation. They are degrading the poor and exploiting them so they can achieve success.

In this world, wealth is inequitably shared. Many millionaires grab all the wealth and leave their brothers and sisters starving for food and thirsty for potable water. We are so unfortunate to grow in a world that has no charity, compassion, and sense of sharing with one another. Our world could be better if the concept of human conscience transcended all the notions of egoism, selfishness, and hatred toward our brothers and sisters. Togetherness is required to lift to construct a better world.

Causes of Poverty in the World

- human disease
- environmental factors / lack of skills
- lack of income / basic services
- inequality / lack of hygiene
- neocolonialism
- dictatorship / lack of water
- social marginalization
- egocentrism/famine
- unemployment
- inequitable resource distribution
- social exclusion
- lack of production
- exploitation
- lack of water and sanitation

Poverty should not exist on this wealthy planet. We are living on a great world, one spotless created by the highest rank of supreme being that has ever existed for all times. That supreme being is God, the sunshine on earth, the provider, and the savior of humanity. We have all the resources to live our lives happily and out of stress and frustration. We have food, water, sunshine, wind, nice vegetation, rivers, nice oceans, plants, and animals that God created to ensure that humanity has adequate goods and resources to survive. As a result, more than half of us are hungry because the resources on earth belong to a category of people.

Our crucial deception on earth is that men failed to understand that we are made of the same human molecules and we are all condemned to live together. The problem of one should be a major concern for another because all of us are traveling on the same boat and on the same road. There are countries in the world in which the death rate is increasing yearly due to lack of medication and lack of doctors to cure them. We must answer to their call. In many countries worldwide, many people spend two to three days at a time without eating because they cannot find anything to feed themselves or their children. We must answer to their call and provide an answer to their request.

One of the dirtiest forms of human indignity is to sell your conscience for materialistic assets. People are trying to get rich by any means, and they do not hesitate to commit any animosity or criminal act to satisfy their own greed and desire. In this world, one cannot trust the other because there is a lack of honesty in every institution. Stealing is going on in every sphere of life. There is stealing in our banks, schools, government offices, and all four corners of the compass.

Poor people are paying more than they consume in gas, electricity, sewer, rents, and mortgages, and there are even more in more cases to complete this list. The people who have wealth and financial resources are not cognizant about the effect of poverty on more than millions of poor people who live on our planet. Starvation, a ubiquitous nightmare in the world, could be eradicated if each country sat together and attempted to bring a solution to the problem. We need to unionize to become not the United States of America but rather the United States of the World. When we are united, we will make progress and altogether rise through prosperity and economic development. The power of unity will illuminate our path toward progress and allow us to see light from the darkness of hell. Our heart, if clean, is our paradise, and our dignity is a passport for all of our accomplishments and successes in life. We must work hard to change the face of earth before it becomes too late.

We are facing great problems with Mother Nature, and our world is on the verge of collapsing and disappearing due to severe natural catastrophic phenomena. Our nature has become violent, and many people are already victimized by seismic catastrophes, tornadoes, and violent hurricanes. We are seeing almost every day some signs of destruction that need to be taken with great attention before things had started degenerating and leading into further complications.

Things are so bad that poverty has become a baleful cause of the mortality rate in the world. Children are starving and cold on the streets. Parents are without work and hungry. There is lack of work and illiteracy. These are all just tiny fish in the great lake of problems that we are facing each day in today's society. God has created us in a paradise land, and we move ourselves to hell. God has paved a straight way for us to follow. We deviated from this road, and we make shortcuts that led us to malediction and curse.

We are tired of seeing murder, abortion, rape, despotism, egoism, racism, exploitation, humiliation, sexism, antisocialism, divorce, imprisonment, pauperism, dictatorship, barbarism, infidelity, social harassment, drug addiction, sickness, favoritism, bias, paganism, and so many other social vicissitudes on our planet.

We must all stand to fight poverty. For people who have not traveled to visit the world, the concept of poverty has no meaning. The real poverty is not in the developed countries. It is rather in some places such as Haiti, Somalia, East Africa, and many other countries in Latin America. Life span is some countries in the world tends to lessen due to poor nutrition and diet and lack of vitamins that our body requires to grow. Malnutrition is a global problem. The major way to stop the course of malnutrition is to first solve the poverty problem.

Hungry children, when they grow older, often have some sort of developmental problem that is directly related to malnutrition. These children also are the objects of abject poverty, humiliation, and malnutrition. The fight to eradicate malnutrition must be implemented in order to lessen malnutrition in the world. People in developed countries tend to have a longer life expectancy rate than they did in the past. It is proven scientifically that malnutrition may cause heart disease, cancer, diabetes, or a poor immune system.

Besides the problem of malnutrition, the earth also has become a jungle. We are not fighting for peace, but we fight to constantly reinforce war and homicide. We are not fighting for justice, but we are battling to promote injustice and exploitation. The world seems to suffer from anger because some people often lose their temper and commit some abominable crime without any apparent causes or reasons. It's hard to understand why terrorists destroy so many lives of innocent people by shooting down an aircraft or bombing a building filled with people, including infants. The power of evils surpasses the power of brotherhood and sisterhood. Our world's moral values are debasing to the lowest point. No one will ever forget the nightmares of September 11 in which so many people died just because they were in the wrong place at the wrong time.

A catastrophe is a dangerous and unexpected situation that faces the society. It affects the economy, political life, security, as well as social life. Crises are never expected. There is always a surprise or threat that creates uncertainties in the world when they occur. Once a crisis occurs, the society may also change as well as the environment sometimes. As a result, many people could be affected physically, mentally, and economically. Any threat to a society always creates a crisis unless it is addressed. Crises may include poverty, economics, environmental, or terrorists/security. This may affect a region, area, or individual as well as an entire nation. The terrorist may have targeted a place where the act would impact many people. Terrorists may conduct many attacks on poor and innocent people. Their attack may be leading to the death of multitudes of people and the destruction of property and valuable assets.

In the event of September 11 attack, approximately three thousand people lost their lives where many were suicide bombers. Over one thousand people who came to rescue people and save lives perished in the attack while many other innocent ones died in the buildings, crushed under rubbles. Many survivors of the attack were severely traumatized and might continue to have psychological or mental problems for quite some time or the rest of their lives. The explosions destroyed many buildings, and such a horrible devastation shook the whole world. The destruction of buildings was also accompanied by the destruction of property worth billions of dollars. With destruction of such magnitude and so many deaths, the family of the fallen people should obtain justice for the victims of the attack.

Emotional crises sometimes change behavioral patterns. Some examples include the following:

- lack of hygiene and neglect
- dramatic change in sleep habits, such a sleeping more often or not sleeping at all
- the loss or gain of weight
- a decline in performance at work or school
- aggressive behavior and attention deficits
- changes in mood, such as irritability, anger, anxiety, or sadness
- a withdrawal from routine activities and isolation

Sometimes these changes happen abruptly and obviously. Events such as a natural disaster or the loss of a job can bring on a crisis in a short period of time. Often though, behavior changes come about gradually. If something doesn't seem right with your loved one, think back over the past few weeks or months to consider signs of change.

The death of a parent can be a sad experience for the children and whole family. The degree of psychological disorder depends on a number of factors, such as the age of both parents and children, the circumstances of the death, the structure of the family, and so on. When a close relative dies, life seems to become nonexistent, and many people need a lot of days to adapt to their normal life after the loss of a relative or close friend. Death is not a punishment. It is the eternal rest. It is the first encounter of man with his Creator to recount on his past life on earth. It is the recovery from pains and sufferings. It is also the end of existence and the day of resurrection.

Coping with the loss of a close friend or family member may be one of the hardest challenges that human beings may face. When we lose a family member such as a spouse, sibling, or parent, our grief can be particularly intense. Loss is understood as a natural part of life, but we can still be overcome by shock and confusion, leading to prolonged periods of sadness or depression. The sadness typically diminishes in intensity as time passes, but grieving is an important process in order to overcome these feelings and continue to embrace the time you had with your loved one.

Everyone reacts differently to death and employs personal coping mechanisms for grief. Research shows that most people can recover from loss on their own through the passage of time if they have social support and healthy habits. It may take months or years to come to terms with a loss. There is no normal time period for someone to grieve. Don't expect to pass through phases of grief either, as new research suggests that most people do not go through stages as progressive steps.

Poverty can cause death as well as disease because our body needs food and fluids to function normally. Based on statistics, about a billion people are going hungry every day, which equals to one-sixth of the world's overall population. The world starvation is currently one of the world's most crucial problems.

On June 19, 2009, the FAO reported 1.02 million people around the world are undernourished. Most live in developing countries. The true cause of starvation has been poor global production, economic crisis, and inflation. There also are various other reasons for lack of food and hunger around the world. Among them are the reasons linked to the weather conditions such as erosion, lack of water, poor global production, pollution, and misuse of natural resources. The problems of hunger and poverty play a great role on people's development and also bring instability and chaos.

Let's talk a little about the misery that is riffing Haiti on a daily basis or without remission. Despite poverty, we love Haiti. The sun of Haiti can attract everyone, even the most difficult people. Haiti was not a garbage can or latrine. Haiti is rather the pearl of the Antilles and the symbol of freedom for all people on earth. All of us are living in the land of Haiti. We have never forgotten the bravery of our heroes like Dessalines, Christophe, Petion, and so forth.

The person who drafted this book is a typical Haitian who loves his flag and all the picturesque sites in his native land. Souvenirs from the alma mater haunt all Haitians who have Haitian blood in their veins. Despite the distance, the freshness and breeze of Haiti has been continuing to blow our hearts and spirits. We cannot erase in our memory the images of children dying of hunger. The tireless workers, like my mother, travel every day in vehicles that are never inspected or pass safety road tests. We will forever keep images of families without children roaming the streets without shoes, pants, and shirts. We want to continue to pray for the sick who suffer and could not find medicine or food to help them in their suffering. We are still surprised that our country continues to wallow in misery, dishonor, and shame despite we are hardworking people proud of our identity and therefore consequent to ourselves. We refuse to live on our knees despite the harmful effects of poverty and ignorance in our country.

Haitians must put the interests of the nation before their own interests and work harder to rebuild our nation. That's sad how our country's patriotic love and sense of civic duty tend to disappear to make way for egoism, shame, and dishonor. Haiti does not produce anymore, and the prices of commodities are continuously multiplying at an accelerated rate. Starvation is a worldwide problem, and unsanitary conditions increase diseases not only in Haiti but all over the entire world.

Haiti became a jungle in which hatred and animosity prevent Haitians from rebuilding the pride of their flag and the country of their ancestors. The streets of Port-au-Prince become a cemetery where the bodies parade before our eyes every hour. Life is really different from what it has always been. In prior years, the rain fell heavily. We saw very beautiful, multicolored butterflies. We saw everywhere the green of our gardens, and we observed migratory birds, especially during the spring season. All these good things have disappeared with time. The most beautiful things always have the worst fate. Our nature is in rebellion, and even the land no longer produces as it did before.

The largest employer in the underdeveloped country is the government. Politics has become a profession, even for those who have not received an elementary education. In Haiti they never give priority to those who are qualified and well trained intellectually to lead the nation. All the people who aspire to run for public buildings have a single objective, to make a fortune and not bring a change in the affairs of the state. For this reason, the millionaires get richer and the poor poorer.

We inherited the colonial mentality of almost all countries that were occupied by either the French or Spanish. This colonialist mentality has created a sense of total dependency. Let us be ourselves as much as possible since it is impossible to move forward if one is under the tutelage of another nation. Our ancestors freed Haiti. We must remain free and independent and raise the Haitian flag above to retain our pride and dignity.

Life is not easy, especially in Third World countries. There are still countries on our planet where people live like animals and have nothing to eat or drink. They walk without a shirt or pants in the streets because they have no clothes to wear. Many people live without seeing a doctor even once in their life. We must all work together to address the misdeeds of extreme poverty. We must have more proximity among peoples who inhabit the earth.

The problem of someone should be the problem of another. Life is worth nothing, but nothing is worth a life. We must live together if we want to progress. Unity is strength. We must stop making war. Neither causes it without any justifiable reasons. It's sad to see people who were killed in the Iraq War, especially the innocent and young children. One must be respected and honored. Life is a divine privilege, and a gift falls from the sky. We must live in peace without fear because the earth does not belong to anyone. We are equal before God, and we should do His will because we are a divine creature.

The ethical values are endangered nowadays, and moral values are nonexistent. Today's children will hardly care about their parents. They have no social formation, and they are almost all immature, malformed, and poorly educated, mentally and socially. The church no longer preaches morality. The shepherds of the church become wolves, and some contribute to the diversion of youth by making sexual statements and engaging in adultery and homosexuality.

For some time, children of the Caribbean could serve as a model for others because of their social and educational training. Today the mentality is different, and bad manners merely multiply, so parents lose their children's control. Children are above all, and they refuse to follow their parents' instructional orders. Such a sick attitude is an incurable disease, and it is a difficult wound to heal. Most children are so corrupt that they do not hesitate to kill their parents for money or material things they would eagerly want to buy as gold and diamonds.

Life on earth is transient. Man is an aggregate of molecules that can be broken in an instant. This transition requires much reflection about our existence on this earth. Plato said very well, "It is good death that ends the sufferings of men on earth." Human perfection does not exist. Man is like a monkey, and sometimes we wonder if the animals would not behave or perform better if they had all our capacities of mental and psychological reasoning. As a cliché said, "We must help each other. It's the law of nature." If we do not live together, we are condemned to live like idiots, and we make our world a jungle and a hell eternally execrable.

In this life, it seems that everything is possible and nothing is impossible. The opportunity to work positively in this life is always conditional, and this conditionality depends always on money and interest. Money is the great Satan that can divide and unite most people who live on this earth. Love for money or material things can cause fraud, divorce, death, family division, adultery, theft, juvenile delinquency, dictatorship, prostitution, betrayal, mental illness, or psychological stress due to too much mental and cerebral concentration.

It is painful to see honest people who work hard every day and are unable to provide for their families or make hot bread at home for their children starving all day. There are people who go to sleep on the floor because they do not have a bed to rest on.

We have problems to see that those who work the most are not always those who have received the most salary. We have seen people who have spent their entire life studying for a profession, but their salary is less than a person who has never been to school. We have examples like rappers, basketball players, and businesspeople who have become multimillionaires without ever having been to school. The global sharing system is false. Our children are not motivated to go to school. They have no model of famous men like in the time of Jean-Jacques Dessalines, Christophe, and Petion.

CORNER OF POETRY

Poor of the World

World, my world, my alma mater
You have plenty; you give plenty
We receive less; we receive plenty
Some of us bless; they have in abundance
Some unfortunate ones have nothing
They live in abject poverty and misery
The rich has seen the blue sky with vivid natural colors
The sky is black and cloudy for some, despite their will and work
The plight of the poor tends to reach its highest peak
Many poor are starving and sick
The heart of the rich gets stronger
The poor hearts languish and suffer
Children are crying and failing
Our humanity is collapsing and praying

World, my world, my alma mater
Our voice is weak; our eyes are blind
We are not mute, but our voice is shutting down
We are hungry; we have no bread
We are thirsty; we have no water

World, my world, my alma mater
We are kneeling down and invoking the name of Jesus
To him the glory, the joy, and the everlasting love
In the name of the Father, the Son, and the Holly Spirit

Homage to Mom

Sleep, Mom, in peace. Sleep on a golden bed
Sleep in a peaceful world, a world with no sorrow, with no
sufferings
A world with no hatred, racism, and discrimination

Sleep, Mom. Sleep in peace. You are still alive in our souls
Your heart is your paradise, and your hell is your short
passage on earth

Sleep, Mom, in peace. Sleep on a golden pillow
Sleep with one eye open and the other eye open on us
Sleep and inspire us with your secret of success
Sleep and remind us to be hardworking and sharing with others
Your dream is our dreams, and our dreams are your dreams

Sleep, Mom. You are very tired after breeding honorably three children
Your role of both father and mother lightens up the world
You are an icon, sunshine, and a golden soul

Sleep, Mom, in peace. Your diamond heart is still running with pride
Mom, your spirits will never die, and your love for us is everlasting
Our hope stands steadfast that one day, Mom,
We will see the golden place that you have been preparing for us
RIP.

ABOUT THE AUTHOR

MAX ALPHONSE CINEUS WAS BORN AND raised in Haiti, where he lived until 1980. Haiti is geographically located in the Caribbean. Many people travel in the Caribbean islands, one of the most exciting places to visit in the world, every year. One of these islands is Hispaniola, which is both the countries of Haiti and the Dominican Republic. Hispaniola has a good record of history, special resources, and very beautiful sites to visit. The general facts, past history, and culture all affect the ways of this country.

The Caribbean Sea is just south of the Gulf of Mexico. The Haitian capital is Port-au-Prince, which is located very close to the island of La Gonave. Haiti's culture is very much like that of the French. In fact Haiti is the only Latin American country where the culture is French. The first language is French, but another common language spoken there is Creole. Many of the people speak Creole because the French settlers introduced this language to them. Creole is a mix of French and the native language that was spoken on the island.

Max left Haiti in the 1980s and immigrated to Montreal (Canada) to study agronomics/agriculture. After a year, he moved to the United States in 1981. There, he lived in Brooklyn (New York) from 1981 to 2000. From 2000 to 2005, Max lived in Queens with his nuclear family. Max is currently living in East Vineland, after moving from Galloway, New Jersey, in 2008.

Having made his decision to move to the United States, Max dropped out of law school to make his migration dream came true. Despite much of the chagrin of his relatives, Max had to leave Haiti and enter the United States to pursue his educational goals and careers. Max is a nationalist who has never backed up any conservative doctrines or neocolonialist ideology. Therefore, he rebuffed the terror of the Duvalier's era, especially under the political regime of Jean-Claude "Baby Doc" Duvalier in which political instability, oppression, unemployment, and violation of human rights were at their maximum level.

During the 1980s, there was poverty, environmental degradation, violence, and instability, and all these crucial problems delayed Haiti's march toward progress, freedom, and development. At the moment this page was being written came the news that Baby Doc had died of a heart attack at the age of sixty-three. He did not receive a state funeral. The opposition groups and the victimized people of his torturous regime felt that a man accused of corruption and mass killings like "Baby Doc" Duvalier did not deserve such an honor. It was a sad day for the Tonton Macoutes, a group of murderers created to provoke mass killings and genocide to terrorize people in rebellion to the regime.

Living in the United States has provided the writer with opportunities to grow and develop, both in his personal and professional life. As a child growing up in the village of Gros-Morne, Max was very fortunate to attend elementary and high school in private institutions despite being the child of a single parent. His father passed away when he was four years old. Max was not aware of the illness that had killed his dad.

The Catholic private schools professed a strong educational and ethical philosophy that has remained with Max throughout his life. Max graduated from Les Frères de l'Instruction Chrétienne around 1966. This foundation—along with the continued support of his late mother, Philomene, some educators, some friends, and his two siblings—allowed him to successfully achieve his dream of becoming an educator, one of the best dedicated to his profession in today's competitive world.

Max married Edith Allen on August 13, 1988, with full attendance of family and friends. It was one of the most important events in his life. Max's mom attended the wedding, and everyone in the family enjoyed that happy day in his life. After some crucial moments of hardships, his older child, Kesha, was born. Then Edwin was born six years after. The births of Kesha and Edwin provided turning points in his life, which triggered him to make the conscious decision to finish college and embark onto a teaching career.

Max's dream was to become a teacher, a cherished dream that came true in 2002. The year 1995, his graduation year at Brooklyn College in New York City, was the best year of his life. He successfully completed his teaching practicum and obtained his bachelor of arts degree. Two years later, he obtained his master of arts degree at Queens College of the City University of New York in the area of languages (liberal arts).

Max also graduated cum laude in social services at Cumberland County College in Vineland, New Jersey. Max also has an extensive knowledge in medical billing and coding. He also studied electronic engineering at the Technical Career Institute in New York.

Max taught in many public schools in New York and New Jersey, including MS 24, MS 167, MS 76, PS 84, PS 199, Egg Harbor Middle School, and Galloway Middle School. And he taught at the New Jersey Labor Department in Cumberland County One Stop Career. He worked at the Bronx Family Court and the Neighborhood Youth Social Services in the Bronx as a counselor. He is currently enrolled as a professor of foreign languages at Salem Community College in Carneys Point, New Jersey. Max obtained his teaching certificate in 2005 in New Jersey. He was nominated for Teacher of the Year in 2002 with an honorific acknowledgment and award recognition.

Printed in the United States
By Bookmasters